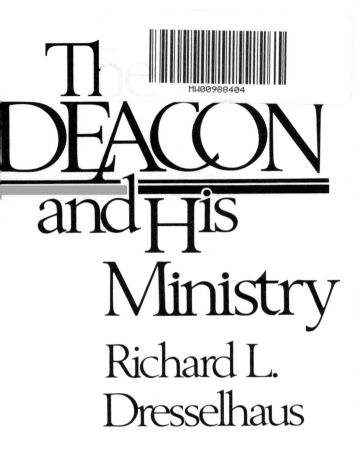

The
DEACON
and His
Ministry

Richard L.
Dresselhaus

GOSPEL PUBLISHING HOUSE
SPRINGFIELD, MISSOURI
02-0493

16th Printing 2006

Scripture quotations marked (NASB®) are taken from the New Ameri●
Standard Bible®, Copyright © 1960, 1962, 1963, 1968, 1971, 1972, 1●
1975, 1977, 1995 by the Lockman Foundation. Used by permission.
(www.Lockman.org)

Library of Congress Catalog Card Number 77-73518
International Standard Book Number 0-88243-493-4

Printed in the United States of America

INTRODUCTION

It is hoped that this manual will meet a real need in every church. Since positive action demands capable and prepared leadership, it is fitting that something be done to help train our laymen to become effective deacons.

The manual is written with the accent on practicality. The issues raised are those which typically confront the deacon board. It is hoped that deacons will find here the kind of help that will prepare them for the challenge of ministering to the church.

Each chapter is designed to serve as a study unit. Suggestions are given for group interaction and problem-solving opportunities. A pastor may wish to lead his deacon board through the manual over a 6-week period, using one chapter per week.

The first chapter presents the Biblical basis for the ministry of the deacon. Outlined here, too, are some of the basic principles for effective spiritual leadership. These are given early since they undergird so much of what is said later in the text.

Chapter 2 deals with the New Testament qualifications for deacons. The list includes those given for elders and bishops as well. A pastor may wish to stretch this chapter into several sessions.

In chapter 3 the deacon is viewed in his work as an administrator. Practical suggestions are offered (for example: agendas, procedures, reports, portfolios, etc.). In some instances you will find help in setting up forms and reporting systems.

The role of the deacon as a servant is outlined in chapter 4. Since the deacon's main task is to serve, it is in order that some of the specific areas of service be dealt with. Visitation, ushering, counseling, and Communion service are typical of the areas considered here.

Since the deacon is first a man of God, the fifth chapter is set aside to discuss the devotional and personal life of the deacon. What does a "devotional relationship" with God involve? How can a deacon encourage his family to participate in "family worship"? What place does the deacon's wife have in his ministry?

The last chapter is designed to give the deacon an opportunity to face life situations typical of those that will confront him in his ministry. It is hoped that this chapter will gather together the principles of effective spiritual leadership outlined in the earlier chapters and set them against the challenge that he now faces as a deacon.

CONTENTS

1

THE MINISTRY OF DEACONS

You have been called to a high place of service in the church of Jesus Christ . . . the Lord has singled you out to be a deacon.

Congratulations!

And now the work begins—agendas, leaky roofs, parliamentary procedure, disgruntled members, balance sheets, and building programs—it is all a part of the job.

But you will enjoy it! Few offices in the church provide such a golden opportunity to do something significant for the kingdom of God.

Paul said to Timothy: "If any man aspires to the office of overseer, it is a fine work he desires to do" (1 Timothy 3:1, *NASB*). The same could be said for a deacon. Yours is a coveted position, and rightly so.

We begin with a survey of the role of the deacon as we find it delineated in the New Testament.

The Church Defined

The deacon's ministry is unto the Lord, but it is carried out within the context of the local church.

Two words must be defined:

(1) *Kuriakos:* This is the Greek word from which we get the English word *church*. It means "belonging to the Lord."

(2) *Ekklesia:* This is the Greek word that is used repeatedly in the New Testament to signify the "assembly" of God's people. The word literally means "the called-out ones."

The Birth of the Church

When was the Church born? This is a question asked by scholars down through the centuries. Some say that the Church had its birth with the Ascension. Others argue convincingly for its birth at Pentecost.

Jesus spoke of the Church in Matthew 16:18 and 18:17, but in these passages He seems to suggest that its birth is yet future. Perhaps Jesus was speaking prophetically of that group of believers who would at a later time form His body, the Church.

When we come to the Book of Acts the picture becomes clear. Here the references point to a local gathering of believers who have come together for worship and instruction (Acts 5:11; 13:1; 18:22). Note, too, that Paul sent his epistles to specific groups of people in designated geographic areas.

The Church clearly has two sides: (1) the invisible side, which includes believers from every place and from every age, and (2) the visible church, which includes the local gathering of believers as they come together for worship and instruction.

The Nature of the Church

The church of Jesus Christ is an organism, a "holy temple in the Lord," and "a habitation of God through the Spirit" (Ephesians 2:20-22). It is the bride of Christ, the body of Christ, and the fellowship of the saints. It draws its life from its Head, the Lord Jesus Christ.

It is to the Church that the deacon is called. He loves

the Church, is committed to its members, and is devoted to its mission. Every facet of its work is in the sphere of his concern.

Following are several implications of this truth for the deacon:

(1) He always speaks well of the Church, knowing it is the body of Christ.

(2) He has his heart set to serve the Church and see it prosper in every way.

(3) He uses every resource to avoid schism and division—and the ridicule and reproach that they bring.

(4) He loves the Church, as Christ loves the Church, and is willing to give his life for her.

The Leadership of the Church

Jesus did not leave His church without leadership. Arising out of the New Testament narrative is a structure of organization that served the Church well in the first century. Under properly appointed leaders, the Church moved forward in unity and strength.

Leadership Defined

(1) *Elders:* When churches were set in order during the first century, elders (*presbuteros*) were appointed to conduct the affairs of the local church (Acts 14:23). Literally, the word meant "older men."

(2) *Bishop:* The term *bishop* (*episkopos*) was used interchangeably with the term *elder* (Acts 20:17, 28). Literally, the word meant "overseer." It may be that the designation *elder* referred to the individual, while the term *bishop* referred to his office.

(3) *Deacon:* The term *deacon* (*diakonos*) was used to designate one who was chosen to serve the

members of the church. He was by definition a servant. Paul called himself a servant, or "deacon," in 1 Corinthians 3:5 and Ephesians 3:7. Even Jesus was said to be a servant, or "deacon," according to Romans 15:8 and John 12:26. Paul told Timothy to be a good servant, or "deacon" (1 Timothy 4:6).

Patterns for Today

The Early Church had two offices to govern its affairs—the office of bishop/elder and the office of deacon. The elder/bishop was concerned with the general oversight of the work, while the deacon was called to serve in practical areas of ministry to the body.

In many churches the eldership is held by the pastor or pastoral staff, and the lay leadership of the church is vested in the board of deacons. However, more recently, some churches have appointed a board of elders to serve the spiritual needs of the membership. The elders give themselves to prayer, ministry to the sick, counseling, and the discipline of members. The deacon board, in these cases, is then free to handle the more practical matters that concern the operation of the church. This does not mean, however, that the deacons ignore the spiritual needs of the church.

In this manual, it will be assumed that the pastor fulfills the role of elder/bishop, while the men who comprise the official board fulfill the role of deacons. It should be noted further that in most churches the deacons act as the trustees of the church. In fact, some boards have an internal division—some men are elected as deacons and some are elected as trustees. Throughout this manual the "official board" will simply be termed "the board of deacons."

Duties of Deacons

The New Testament is not as explicit as we might like when it comes to a practical definition of the role of the deacon. What were the duties of the deacons who served in the Early Church? Who were the deacons? What were their specific duties? What was the manner of their selection and the tenure of their office? These questions press for answers that are not easy to find. A scriptural survey follows below:

(1) Philippians 1:1—Paul addresses this epistle to the bishops and deacons who were in the church at Philippi. The reference only tells us of the existence of their office well on into the second half of the first century.

(2) 1 Timothy 3:8-10, 12, 13—Here Paul sets forth the qualifications for the office of deacon, but says nothing about their duties and responsibilities. We may properly assume that the office is generally recognized in the church by this time, but we are left in the dark as to its duties. First Timothy bears a slightly later date than the Book of Philippians.

(3) Romans 16:1—This reference pushes us closer to the birth of the Church, but helps little to define the role of deacons in the Early Church. However, if by this rather early date the church had appointed a deaconess, it seems logical that the office of deacon was also known.

(4) Acts 6:1-6—Many see in this passage the New Testament pattern for what the church today calls the office of deacon. Seven men were chosen to "wait on tables," thus freeing the apostles to carry on their ministry without hindrance.

It should be noted, however, that these appointed servants are not referred to as "deacons." And, further, two of them, Philip and Stephen, became preachers of the gospel in only a short time.

Early Fathers

The Early Church fathers shed some light on the role of deacons in the church of the first few centuries:

(1) Ignatius: This man, a contemporary of John the Apostle, states that the deacons were not mere servers of meat and drink. The inference here is that the role of the deacon was becoming a recognized office in the church by the end of the first century.

(2) Irenaeus: The church in Irenaeus' day saw a clear pattern in Acts 6 and believed that the church should be under the direction of not more than seven men.

(3) Council of Neo-Caesarea: In A.D. 315 this council set seven as the accepted number for the group of men who administered the affairs of the church.

Conclusions

The New Testament is unclear about the actual duties and functions of the deacons. However, judging from the composite of scriptural references and the testimony of the Early Church fathers, it is reasonably clear that the Early Church was served by a group of committed men who were called deacons, and that it was their duty to serve the church in whatever capacity those circumstances dictated.

Variations of the word *diakoneo*, "to serve," are found over 100 times in the New Testament. Repetition points to emphasis. The Early Church saw the need for selected individuals to serve the body of Christ in practical matters.

In summary, the following inferences may be drawn:

(1) The deacon was appointed to serve the church in any area of need that might arise.

(2) The deacon was called to a supportive role in the spiritual ministry of the church.

(3) The effectiveness of the deacon's service was determined by the measure of his commitment and faithfulness.

(4) The deacon was expected to serve the church by the example of his character as well as by his deeds.

The Deacon Today

What can be said to help deacons become equipped for the task that faces them in today's church? Are there basic principles of Christian living that will help them be the kind of leaders God wants them to be? Isn't there a way to avoid those nasty pitfalls that so often claim the efforts of good men?

Yes, there are basic principles of Christian living that have special impact upon the men chosen of the Lord to lead His church. Some of them are listed here. They are basic principles to guide the deacon in his calling as a spiritual leader:

(1) *Serve in the power of the Spirit.* It has been suggested that man is tripartite—he has a body, soul, and spirit. The body is that part that is seen and felt—the head, the legs, the heart. The soul is that part that is unseen but yet very real—it has to do with the personality, the emotions, the will, and the intellect—all those things that produce individuality. The spirit is also unseen, but, most important, it is the place of communion with God.

The question here has to do with the level we function on in our service for God. Some men are motivated to serve God for primarily selfish reasons of gain. They hope to get rich; to make a sumptuous living doing God's work.

Other men serve on the soulish level. They seek to make their mark by the power of their intellect, the force of their will, or the persuasion of their personality.

Unfortunately, too many of God's people live on this level. They are Christian humanists. They attempt to do God's work with might and power. The accent is on what they can do more than on what God can do.

The third level is the spirit level. Might and power are made to yield to a higher principle—the working of the Spirit.

Most of us have attempted to do God's work by vacillating back and forth between the second and third levels. We draw on all our human resources and set out to build the Kingdom. When that fails, we finally admit that only the Spirit can enable us to do the work of the Lord.

The word *charismatic* is important at this point. When broken into its etymological parts it means "active grace" or "flowing grace." It simply means that the believer is but a channel through which God works by His Spirit. Pentecostal people are the people of the "flow through." The gifts and ministries of the Spirit flow out through their lives in blessing to the world.

Think of the tension that could be alleviated in the church if this principle were lived out. Think of the difference it would make as the deacon board grapples with the weighty issues of church leadership.

God has called you to be a deacon. Learn first that it is not by might or by power, but it is by the Spirit. It is a principle you cannot afford to violate in the work of God.

(2) *Spiritual growth comes through conflict.* A preacher once asked: "How does a Christian grow?" Then he paused.

While he paused I began to answer . . . inside myself: "By reading the Bible, through witnessing, by being faithful in worship. . . ."

Then he answered with but one word: "Conflict."

I have thought about it often. And I have experienced the power of the truth repeatedly. It really is true. We grow through conflict.

On the surface it would seem to be good if we could enjoy perpetual tranquillity. But would we grow? What makes a tree strong? What factors worked together to make Paul the man of faith that he became? If you took the conflict out of Peter's life, would you ever get the kind of man described in the Book of Acts? I think not.

We grow by conflict!

This may seem like an obvious principle, but it really works. It is when we find ourselves "in a rub" that we see how needy we are and how much we need God's grace.

It is when someone makes you wait that you see how impatient you are.

It is when someone falsely accuses you that you see how vindictive you are.

It is when someone won't let you have your way that you see how stubborn you are.

It is when someone ignores you that you see how insecure you are.

Conflict drives us to our knees and compels us to live near to the Cross. Out of exposed need flows repentance and forgiveness. Conflict is the key.

Deacons have a golden opportunity to grow, for they will meet conflict along the way of service. If the deacon resists conflict, seeing it as negative and insulting, he will crumble under the responsibilities that are his. If he sees conflict as a positive opportunity for growth, he will note with appreciation the spiritual growth in his own life and the enhancing value of his contribution to the work of God.

It will help you to remember that the cross is the place of conflict, but it was the occasion for the greatest of victories.

Obviously, do not seek conflict, but rejoice when it inevitably comes and learn to view it as a positive force that will move you on toward spiritual growth.

Growth comes through conflict!

(3) *Keep your sword in the sheath.* Peter had every reason to use his sword on the servant of the high priest. Was not his Lord and Master being threatened with death? He had every "right" to fight back—or did he?

Most of us "fight for our rights." We draw a circle of defense around us and challenge anyone to step foot across the line. We contend for what we understand to be our personal rights. If our toe gets stepped on, we seek revenge—our rights have been violated.

Jesus proved by example the force of this principle. He had every right in heaven and on earth to call down the angels and destroy the Roman soldiers that stripped Him bare of all self-respect and decency. But He didn't. He laid aside His rights as a man that He might fulfill the "right . . . eousness" of the Father.

And we are called to do the same. As a spiritual leader you will be called upon to lay aside what could be clearly understood as your personal rights in order to meet a higher demand of service.

You will need to hold your temper when you have every "right" to speak.

You will be called upon to serve beyond the limits of logic and fairness.

You will be confronted repeatedly with the privilege of honoring others above yourself.

You will need to lay down your life, and its "right," to be a reflection of the One whom you serve.

Peter missed the mark. All he had to show for his "pay-back" attitude was a severed ear. And the last miracle that Jesus did before the crucifixion was to put it back in its place.

And be sure of this: If you fight for your "rights," your trophies of victory will be no better than that of Peter.

Spiritual leaders are called to lay down their own rights so the "righteousness" of Jesus might be known.

(4) *Live in the light.* First John 1:7 says: "If we walk in the light as He himself is in the light, we have fellowship with one another, and the blood of Jesus His Son cleanses us from all sin" *(NASB).*

The temptation is to live in isolation—to pull up inside our shell and stay as hidden as possible. John says it ought not to be so with Christians. We are to walk in the light of divine revelation, and that involves horizontal as well as vertical relationships.

Too often suspicions and surmisings overcome the light of love and openness. Walls of misunderstanding and distrust are built. The people of God give themselves over to base feelings of vindictiveness and animosity, and the work of God falters.

The call of the Spirit is that the people of God live together in the light of Christ's love and grace. And spiritual leaders are to set the pace. As a deacon you are under obligation to live transparently and openly before those whom you lead. If you are to call others into the light, you must first dwell there yourself.

A deacon board that adopts this principle as a practical guideline will find that their relationships together will be enhanced and their leadership among the people will be strengthened.

One of the most powerful prayers that a Christian can pray is this: "Let the Spirit of truth prevail." Since Jesus is Truth, it is in obeying Him that we find the answer to this prayer unfolding before us. We will, as John said, have true fellowship as we live together in light and love.

(5) *Dare to admit wrong.* Board meetings have been deadlocked, churches split, and pastors sent on their way because no one was willing to admit he was wrong.

In principle, the follower of Christ knows that he is by nature wrong—wrong in his attitudes, wrong in his motives, wrong in his deeds. This is why he needs God's continual grace. Though not sinning willfully, he is always conscious of his shortcomings and finds that by admitting his basic wrongness he receives the abundant flow of God's grace.

Apply this to the ministry of the deacon. He never forgets his own vulnerability—he is never above error and he should always be open to an examination of his position. However, his openness does not in any way reflect indecisiveness but instead an awareness of his own basic nature. In other words, he approaches his ministry in a spirit of deep humility.

Always be prepared to say: "I could be wrong."

(6) *Forgive before you are asked to forgive.* When Jesus said from the cross, "Father, forgive

them," there was no one in that crowd that was asking Him to forgive. Yet, He did! And we must, too.

Some have called it "unilateral forgiveness," an extension of forgiveness that makes no demands on an erring brother.

A positive power is released when we do this. Just try it! Forgive a brother, in your heart, while he is still at work to harm you. When you meet him again, you will find a tranquillity of spirit that will communicate life to him. And, hopefully, prompt him to repentance.

How sad and tragic when men in God's work hold grudges, waiting for others to produce "fruit worthy of repentance." No one gives! The air gets tense. And months and years pass, waiting for someone to forgive first.

This principle brings freedom to spiritual leaders and puts them in a place where they can be greatly used to minister truth and love even to those who wrong them.

There are a host of equally valid and useful "life principles" that could be mentioned. But if spiritual leaders will consider even just these and do them, God's work will feel the positive impact.

Again, congratulations! You have been called to serve in a high place. And the smaller you feel the bigger that place will become.

You, too, can say: "I can do all things through Christ who strengthens me!" (Philippians 4:13).

Suggestions for Group Study

(1) Discuss: The operation of the church today must adapt itself to correct administrative procedures consistent with our times. The New Testament is a guide in spiritual matters but not necessarily in or-

ganizational matters. In other words, just because the Early Church had deacons does not mean that the church today should have deacons. Maybe there is a more "streamlined" way of doing things.

(2) Illustrate: Try to find illustrations that will show how the "life principles" listed in the text work in everyday living. Has anyone ever tried to work with someone who could never be wrong? Has anyone experienced the effects of "unilateral forgiveness"?

(3) Apply: What can be gleaned from this chapter to make your work as a deacon more effective?

2

THE QUALIFICATIONS FOR DEACONS

The New Testament presents a list of qualifications for elders, deacons, and bishops. Here we will put the lists together and come up with a composite of qualifications for spiritual leaders.

Gene A. Getz, in *The Measure of a Man*, lists these qualifications.[1] We will use his choice of terms for each qualification given by the apostle Paul.

Paul does not mince words when he lays down the requirements for spiritual leaders. As you go through these qualifications, you will likely feel very inadequate and dependent on the Lord. In fact, you may wonder how you were chosen to be a spiritual leader. But don't forget, the Lord sees your heart. It is not so much what you are now but what you will become that matters most to Him.

Here, then, are the qualifications and requirements for men who lead the church:

(1) *Above reproach* (1 Timothy 3:2). The emphasis here, as well as in Titus 1:6, 7 and Acts 6:3, is on a man's reputation. How is he regarded by those who personally know him? The believers in Lystra reported to Paul that Timothy "was well spoken of by

---

[1] Gene A. Getz, *The Measure of a Man: A Practical Guide to Christian Maturity* (Glendale, CA: Gospel Light Regal Publications, 1974).

the brethren who were in Lystra and Iconium" (Acts 16:2). A spiritual leader must have a good reputation. His positive impact on God's work will demand it.

A nominating committee, when evaluating nominees for the office of deacon, should make inquiry about his known reputation. How do people who work side by side with him day after day feel about him? Is he regarded highly in his community? How does his family feel about him?

(2) *Husband of one wife* (1 Timothy 3:2). The Roman culture of Paul's day was accentuated with moral looseness much like we have in our day. In 1 Corinthians 5:1 Paul states that the immorality of the pagan culture had not only gotten into the church but had demonstrated itself in ways too shameful even for the pagans to comprehend. It is against this background that Paul writes.

Paul concludes that a man must be married to only one woman—and we might add, be living with her in tranquillity, peace, and fulfillment.

Some spiritual leaders have failed at this point. Unable to cope with the many temptations facing men today, they fall into sin. Satan delights in robbing a man of spiritual authority by bringing him down in this area.

Gene Getz provides five powerful guidelines:

(a) We must develop good communication with our wives.

(b) We should not set up conflict situations by deliberately exposing ourselves to temptation.

(c) We should fortify ourselves through regular study of the Word of God and prayer.

(d) We must avoid unnecessary idleness.

(e) We should seek help from someone we can trust if the problem seems beyond our control.

(3) *Temperate* (1 Timothy 3:2). The Greek word behind this qualification for spiritual leaders means "free from excess, passion, ruckus, confusion, etc., . . . well-balanced, self-controlled."[2] A spiritual leader is well-oriented mentally, socially, spiritually, and physically.

The power of God extends to every area of living. It is God's purpose, in Christ, to bring a man into harmony with himself, with the world in which he lives, and at peace within himself. This is a "temperate" man—usable to God in spiritual leadership.

(4) *Prudent* (1 Timothy 3:2; Titus 1:8). Since this word in the original has a degree of ambiguity as to its meaning, it is helpful to see Paul's use of the same word in Romans 12:3. Here Paul admonishes the Roman believer "not to think of himself more highly than he ought to think; but to think soberly. . . ." The Greek word translated "soberly" in Romans 12 is the same word Paul uses in 1 Timothy and Titus, but here it is translated "prudent."

The point is clear. A spiritual leader is to be humble, willing to serve others, and accurate in his view of himself. He must never forget that he is what he is only by the grace of God.

(5) *Respectable* (1 Timothy 3:2). The Holy Spirit is very practical. Here He inspires Paul to speak of the importance of living a well-ordered life. The word *kosmios*, in its root form, means to "put in order . . . adorn, decorate."[3] A spiritual leader is careful about his dress, the cleanliness of his office, the knot in his tie, the dress of his children, the paint on his house, and the greenness of his lawn.

---

[2] William F. Arndt and F. Wilbur Gingrich, *Greek-English Lexicon of the New Testament,* 4th rev. ed. (Chicago: University of Chicago Press, 1957).

It really matters! The world gets a better view of Christ when they see by the manner in which we live that we really do care. Love comes out best that way!

(6) *Hospitable* (1 Timothy 3:2; Titus 1:8). Leviticus 19:33, 34 stands behind this New Testament directive: "When a stranger resides with you in your land, you shall not do him wrong. The stranger who resides with you shall be to you as the native among you, and you shall love him as yourself . . ." (NASB).

What is your attitude toward your home? Have you given it to Christ for His use as He leads? A spiritual leader views hospitality not just as a social grace, but as a way of bringing others into an atmosphere of love and Christian concern.

(7) *Able to teach* (1 Timothy 3:2; Titus 1:9). All of us know individuals who are well-informed, articulate, and gifted in the art of communications. Yet this qualification for spiritual leadership has more to do with manner and quality of life than with special gifts of expression.

The word translated by this phrase "able to teach" (*didaktikos*) is also used by Paul in 2 Timothy 2:24. There the word is grouped with other designations that clearly refer to quality and manner of life. Paul says that the servant of the Lord is not to be quarrelsome, but to be kind, forbearing, and gentle. All this is inferred in the word here translated "able to teach."

This point is powerful. A spiritual leader is to communicate Christ with his entire life. His attitude, industry, integrity, and behavior all speak of his devotion to Christ. In other words, he teaches by example! He is an epistle of truth and life! Men can look his

---

[3] *Ibid.*

24

way and see Christ. What a man does in this sense is more powerful than what he says.

(8) *Not addicted to wine* (1 Timothy 3:2, 3; Titus 1:7). The word used here *(paroinos)* means to "over-drink," or to be "addicted" to wine. Although the reference here is not to total abstinence, the Bible elsewhere is very explicit in its warnings about the use of alcoholic beverages. (Note especially Proverbs 23:19-21, 29-34.)

Paul says: "It is good not to eat meat or to drink wine, or to do anything by which your brother stumbles" (Romans 14:21, NASB). In a culture like ours where drunkenness is prevalent, the spiritual leader will do well to avoid any conduct that could cause reproach to the work of God. Paul's admonition to the Ephesians puts the matter in positive perspective: "And do not get drunk with wine, for that is dissipation, but be filled with the Spirit" (Ephesians 5:18, NASB).

(9) *Not self-willed* (Titus 1:7). Here Paul describes the man who lives in the center of his own world. He sees those around him as his servants. Ideas that do not originate with him are quickly repudiated. His spirit is one of control.

An effective spiritual leader is one who works well with others. If he finds an idea that runs counter to his personal desires but is best for the entire group, he willingly accepts it. He puts others before himself and avoids "mind sets." He is a team man who looks at controversial issues with an open, objective mind.

(10) *Not quick-tempered* (Titus 1:7). Paul warns Titus to avoid men who have quick tempers; who are given to sudden outbursts of anger. Sinful anger has its roots in revenge and bitterness. It feeds on resentment. Many times God's work has been hindered by

men who lacked self-control and were easily provoked to destructive expressions of anger.

Words are like feathers. They scatter easily and once scattered are impossible to collect. Outrage releases words of poison that corrupt and destroy whatever they touch. Every spiritual leader must practice self-control. He must rule his spirit and learn to hold his tongue from expressions of anger and vindictiveness. Temper tantrums and spiritual leadership are mutually exclusive.

(11) *Not pugnacious* (Titus 1:7). The King James Version has captured the meaning of the Greek word *plaktan* by translating it "striker," one who physically lashes out at another. Here Paul speaks not of anger verbalized, but of anger out of control physically.

Cain was guilty of this sin, and killed his brother Abel. Moses was guilty of this sin, and killed an Egyptian. Peter was guilty of this sin, and attempted to kill the servant of the high priest.

God calls His servants to humility, self-control, and peace. Vented anger is not to be tolerated.

(12) *Uncontentious* (1 Timothy 3:2, 3). The Greek word that is translated here by the word *uncontentious* is *amaichos*, "peaceable."

Gene Getz tells this story:[4]

> Tom is a smart, outgoing successful businessman. He is president of his own company . . . and is doing well—in fact, very well! . . . Six months ago Tom was elected to serve as an elder in his church, but there was something about Tom that no one really knew. As long as he was "calling the shots" and "making all the decisions," he was happy, easy to live with, and

[4] Getz, *op. cit.*

cooperative. But when he was just one among equals, it was a different story. . . . Tom always seemed to take an opposite point of view from everyone else on the board. If it was his idea, fine! But if the ideas came from someone else, he could never seem to get excited about it. . . . Needless to say, Tom literally destroyed the unity among this group of men. . . . He forced a vote on every issue, which usually came out 8 to 1 against Tom.

The man of God is called to peace and not contention. Unfortunately, Tom had not learned this lesson. The work of God was impaired, and so was his own life.

(13) *Gentle* (1 Timothy 3:2, 3). Here is the antithesis of the three qualities noted above. Paul tells us that the man of God is to be gentle. The original word *epeikais* means "yielding, gentle, kind, forbearing."[5]

All men are called to follow Jesus. He is the model. No man ever demonstrated such a gentle spirit as He. In the midst of mocking, slander, and ridicule, Jesus responded with gentleness and forbearance.

How does a man conduct himself when he is under pressure? When the membership makes unjust and undue demands, what then? In the heat of a tumultuous business session, how does he respond? The only proper answer to each of these questions is: in a spirit of gentleness and forbearance.

(14) *Free from the love of money* (1 Timothy 3:2, 3). The word behind this phrase is *aphilarguron*. It is comprised of three parts: *a*—not; *phil*—love; and *arguron*—silver, money. The admonition is pointed. Paul tells spiritual leaders: "Don't love money!"

Jesus taught: "Where your treasure is, there will

---

[5] Arndt and Gingrich, *op. cit.*

your heart be also" (Matthew 6:21). The man of God must place his treasures under the control of Christ. All that he possesses must be viewed as a God-given resource, given so it might be given back. The work of God is not to be thwarted by leadership that puts riches above the Kingdom and its growth.

(15) *One who manages his own household well* (1 Timothy 3:2-4). The measure of a man is his family. A man who has proven his leadership in the home will likely prove his leadership in the church.

The tragic story of Eli, who refused to restrain his rebellious sons, and David, who contributed to the delinquency of Absalom through apparent neglect, should be a solemn warning to every man of God.

The home is the real test. A man may succeed in business, politics, or education, but be unable to build a strong home. This man is not qualified to serve the Lord as a leader in the church. The standard is high because the responsibility is great. The call is for men who are strong at home and will be strong in the church.

(16) *A good reputation with those outside* (1 Timothy 3:7). The responsibilities of spiritual leaders reach beyond the walls of the church building. They live under the eye of a community at large. And their testimony for Christ must have a clear ring out there as well.

When selecting church leadership, this factor must be weighed. How do his neighbors feel about him? When he is out of town on business, what is the report of his associates there? Can his life-style and manner stand the scrutiny of those outside his circle of close friends? It must!

"Conduct yourselves with wisdom . . . , let your speech always be with grace . . . , keep your behavior excellent . . . , lead a quiet life and attend to your own business . . . , behave properly toward outsiders . . ." (Colossians 4:5, 6; 1 Peter 2:12; 1 Thessalonians 4:11, 12; *NASB*).

(17) *Loving what is good* (Titus 1:7, 8). Some people have an eye for evil. They see the bad, that which is wrong, and those things that ought to be other than they are. But there are others who have an eye trained to spot the slightest good, a bit of positive influence, a ray of light and hope—and these are the ones that God chooses to lead His church.

The Scriptures say that evil is overcome by good (Romans 12:21). The mind is to think on things that are true, honorable, right, pure, lovely, and of good report. As a man thinks, so he is.

Love what is good. The call is for men trained and exercised in this vocation. Men who can look at impossibilities and see the possible, at the hopeless and see hope, and at the fallen and see restoration.

(18) *Just* (Titus 1:7, 8). This is a call for spiritual maturity, for men who have the psychological and spiritual balance to make "just" decisions.

The word *just (dikaios)* may refer to a man in his position of righteousness before God—a just man before God; or it may refer to practical righteousness, as when Joseph is described as a "just man."

In any event, the word suggests to spiritual leaders the imperative of a right vertical relationship with God and a right horizontal relationship with men.

Fairness and equity are necessities for effective spiritual leadership, and God's people have a right to demand its presence in their leaders.

(19) *Devout* (Titus 1:7, 8). The original word here is *hosios*, meaning "devout, pious, pleasing to

God."[6] The accent here is on God's choosing a man's life—he is set aside for the work and pleasure of the Lord. As the furniture in the tabernacle was declared holy unto God, so the man of God is set apart for ministry to God and ministry to men.

The practical holiness of which Paul speaks is not a spirit of isolationism and separatism. The call is away from all that is immediate and of this earth so that the one to whom the call comes may go back into his world and win it to Christ. The most pious —truly pious—are the most involved in reaching lost men for Christ.

(20) *Not a new convert* (1 Timothy 3:6). Paul admonishes Timothy to refrain from choosing new converts *(neophutos)* to fill places of spiritual leadership. His concern is not only for the church but for them. They may become conceited and filled with pride. Or they may become discouraged by the negative pressures that inevitably come.

The walk with God is a walk of growth and development, and it takes time. A new convert, while having great zeal, lacks the depth of understanding and wisdom that flows out of experience. When confronted with the pressures of leadership he will find it difficult to act decisively and wisely.

A caution is in order. This in no way refers to chronological age, nor, in fact, to time itself. Some men have "been in the way" for years, yet are "new converts" in maturity. A man's qualifications for leadership should be weighed according to criteria measuring spiritual growth and development.

The Scriptures hold forth a high standard for spiritual leadership, but that is as it should be, for

[6] *Ibid.*

there is no work on earth so important to time and eternity as the building of Christ's kingdom through His body, the Church.

Suggestions for Group Study

Discuss:

(1) Which of the requirements do you think are the most difficult to satisfy?

(2) How does a deacon handle the problem of feeling unworthy and unqualified to fill this office?

(3) Does God sometimes allow a man to be chosen as a deacon when he has some obvious deficiencies in his life?

(4) Are there some qualifications in the list that you would single out as more important than others?

(5) Are there qualifications you think should be added, or, if you were making out the list, what insertions and exclusions would there be?

Project: Why not set up a program for "self-improvement" in the deacon board? Perhaps the deacons should meet regularly just to take an honest look at themselves in light of these qualifications. By helping each other, they could grow together and receive help in becoming the kind of men God has ordained them to be. Others can usually see our flaws more easily than we can see them.

Illustration: As a group of men, put the apostle Paul against the list of requirements he gives and see how well he matches up to them. Can you find any areas of weakness? What are the obvious points of great strength? Do you feel comfortable knowing that Paul gave these requirements? That is, do you think Paul practiced what he preached?

3

THE DEACON
AS AN ADMINISTRATOR

Something should be said here about the selection of deacons and their term of office, and then a discussion of his role as an administrator will follow.

In most churches one of two methods is used in selecting the deacon board: by a nominating committee or nominations at the annual business meeting.

Selecting a Deacon

(1) A nominating committee, recommended by the pastor and approved by the deacon board, presents in nomination the names of those men whom they feel meet the Biblical qualifications to serve as deacons. The congregation, at its annual business meeting, proceeds in choosing from that list those who should serve. Of course, nominations from the floor are generally accepted.

This method has the strength of careful screening. The nominating committee may wish to interview prospective nominees, or they may work from a carefully prepared questionnaire. In either case, the names that go before the congregation have been prayerfully and thoughtfully chosen. This is a strong plus for this system of selecting deacons.

Following is a list of questions that should be

answered by a nominee before his name is placed in nomination for the office of deacon:

(a) Do you know Christ as your personal Lord and Saviour?

(b) Have you been baptized in the Holy Spirit, and are you living a Spirit-controlled life to the best of your ability?

(c) Do you feel led to serve the Lord as a deacon?

(d) Do you understand that the deacon's ministry is that of service to the body of Christ?

(e) Are you prepared to submit yourself first to the Lord, then to His people, and finally to the other leaders with whom you will work?

(f) Do you support the local church with your tithes and offerings?

(g) Do you agree with the tenets of faith and governing principles of the church to which you belong?

(h) Do you live a life that is consistent with the Word of God as pertains to morality, conversation, life-style, and appearance?

(i) Do you conduct your home life in a way that meets with the demands of Scripture? Do you conduct a regular family altar in your home? Are your children in submission to God and to you as the head of the home?

(j) If chosen, will you serve as a deacon in an attitude of love, unity, and faith?

If diligence is practiced in the selection process, those who are chosen will know that the office to which they are called is one of great importance. Dare the church do less than put forth every effort to choose the right leadership to chart its course and set the pace? God's way is to have the right man in the right place at the right time. This is the key to the building of a great church!

(2) A second method of selecting deacons is to have the congregation both nominate and elect them at its annual business meeting. This method is often used in a smaller congregation where nearly everyone is knowledgeable about the men who qualify for the office of deacon.

The weakness of this method is obvious: it is impossible to screen nominees in a public meeting. Sometimes it is with embarrassment that a nominee must stand and refuse nomination. Or, more tragic than that, a man may be elected who is not qualified to hold the office of deacon.

On the positive side, this method gives the entire congregation the opportunity to be involved in the complete selection process. It prevents the existing board from attempts to propagate itself by carefully choosing men for the nominating committee.

Again, if the congregation is relatively small, this can perhaps be the most effective way of choosing deacons. Every church must evaluate its particular needs and then decide which method it should use.

In any event, great care must be taken in the all-important task of selecting leadership in the church.

The Term of Office

There are two approaches to the term of office for deacons in many churches.

(1) Successive terms: Some churches elect deacons for a 3-year term and upon the completion of that term the deacon may be reelected for another 3-year term.

The strengths are these:

(a) The retention of proven leadership

34

(b) Continuity and uniformity

(c) Stability and permanence

The weaknesses are these:

(a) The monopolization of leadership by a few men

(b) The lack of fresh, new ideas

(c) The difficulty in eliminating poor leadership

(2) Nonsucceeding terms: Other churches elect deacons to a 3-year term. At the completion of that term another man is chosen to fill that office. After 1 year that deacon may be returned to office, but he cannot succeed himself.

Generally speaking, for the reasons noted above, this is the most satisfactory way to handle the term of office for the deacon. Each church will need to decide which method will serve its needs the best.

Assigning Portfolio

A wise pastor will immediately assign specific areas of responsibility to each deacon. He should be careful to match talent with task, and he may find it advantageous to talk to each deacon about his strengths and weaknesses before assigning him an area.

This procedure will free the pastor so he may concentrate on the specific ministry to which he has been called. It will give the deacon an area of service that he understands and that has been defined for him.

The following is an example of the kind of breakdown that can work for a seven-man deacon board:

(1) Building and maintenance

(2) Ushering and Communion

(3) Sunday school

(4) Youth

    (5) Missions

    (6) Stewardship

    (7) Music

Each area should be delineated with enough detail so the deacon will fully understand what is necessary in discharging his responsibilities. Men serve best when they know precisely what is expected of them. A fuzzy job assignment will inevitably result in a slipshod performance.

Another thing to remember is the need for accountability. A pastor who asks for systematic reports will find that performance is greatly enhanced. There is also positive motivational value in demanding accountability. It makes a man feel that his task is important and that someone cares. A wise pastor will devise a reporting system that will give him the needed information and provide the deacon with a way to report the progress achieved in his area.

A sample monthly report form is included here. These completed forms could be collected and discussed at each monthly board meeting:

DEACON'S MONTHLY REPORT
(Missions)

Name (John Jones)

1. What was the gross income in missions for the month of May? ($1,020.16)

2. What is the percentage of increase or decrease over 1 year ago? (13.5%)

3. What future events involving missions should be placed on the church calendar?

    (Convention, Oct. 10-15)

    (District Missions Rally, Sept. 16)

4. What programs do you now envision for the future?

(An educational program)
(Youth motivational seminar)
(All-church missions banquet)

5. Are there areas in your department that need full-board input?

(Underwriting budget for all-church missions banquet; appointment of a new missions secretary)

6. What is your attitude toward your area of responsibility? Do you feel positive about it? Are you enjoying your work?

(I enjoy these responsibilities. The continual growth in missions is gratifying. I would like to see greater interest in home missions.)

Obviously, each portfolio will need its own report form. And each pastor will want to use a form that will reflect the program that he feels is compatible with the church he pastors. However, the above form will give a general guide to those pastors and deacons who choose to use a report form.

The congregation should be informed of the portfolio assignments. When they have questions in a given area, they can go to that deacon rather than seeking out the pastor for the needed information.

It may also be advisable for the deacons to have an opportunity at some time to make a summary report to the entire congregation. The annual business meeting provides a good occasion for this, if the reports are printed and are kept brief.

Deacons' Meeting

The bylaws followed by many churches call for a monthly meeting of the deacon board. Larger churches may need to have additional meetings, as the need demands. And, in any church, matters arise from time to time that will necessitate a special meeting of the board of deacons.

Prior to the meeting, an agenda should be sent to each deacon. With the agenda items available prior to the meeting, the deacon is able to give thought and prayer to each matter before arriving at the meeting. A deacon board will make wiser decisions if they have adequate time to consider each issue ahead of time.

The following is a sample agenda for a typical board meeting:

MONTHLY MEETING OF THE OFFICIAL BOARD
October 16, 7:00 p.m.
Covening in Pastor's Office

1. Devotions (a 5-minute devotional thought by a deacon is good, followed by group prayer and worship)
2. Minutes of last meeting
3. Financial report
4. Reports of deacons
   a. Building and maintenance
   b. Ushering and Communion
   c. Sunday school
   d. Youth
   e. Missions
   f. Stewardship
   g. Music

5. Action on reports
6. New business
   a. The acquisition of playground equipment
   b. Wage adjustments for secretarial staff
   c. The proposed purchase of kitchen equipment
   d. Candidates for membership
   e. Repair of roof over church office
7. Adjournment

Naturally, the agenda will be dictated by the matters that need action. It is not so important what form the agenda takes as it is that there be an agenda. Too often board meetings "freewheel" and unnecessary time is taken. Deacons will learn to appreciate the efforts of the pastor as he attempts to facilitate board action by giving careful thought to the agenda.

Deacon's Notebook

Wise decisionmaking demands the immediate availability of relevant materials. For this reason, every deacon should maintain a notebook that will keep at his fingertips the resources he will need as he discusses and acts on matters that have to do with the operation and ministry of the church.

A loose-leaf notebook is preferable for this purpose. It may be well for the pastor to take the lead in this and provide for each deacon a notebook with the necessary labeled dividers. Suggested divisions are:

(1) Portfolio assignments
(2) Deacon reports
(3) Staff job descriptions
(4) Staff reports
(5) Agendas
(6) Board minutes
(7) Monthly financial reports
(8) Special reports

Each deacon is expected to keep his notebook current. When his term of office expires, he passes the notebook on to his successor. In this way, there is a continuity of information available for the new deacon.

A deacon will take pride in his work if he is trained to be efficient, and the availability of information is the key to making that efficiency possible.

Financial Records

It has already been stated that careful recordkeeping is essential. However, a reminder of the importance of good financial records is in order.

The members of the congregation deserve to know how the finances of the church are being handled. A system must be devised that is workable, easily understood, and has "expansion potential" as the church grows. A professional system should be sought to be sure that the system being used is proper.

The Internal Revenue Service is becoming far more stringent in their requirements for nonprofit organizations. No church should give an occasion for questions to be raised. Sound principles of accounting are essential.

General Observations

It may be helpful to mention several matters that assist the deacons in their work together as a board:

(1) Follow the accepted rules of parliamentary procedure. This will assure fairness in the decision-making process and will eliminate needless waste of time.

(2) Be guided by a spirit of cooperation. The board of deacons should function as a team. "Unity amid diversity" must be a practical principle.

(3) Maintain clear and complete records of action taken at any regular or special meeting of the board of deacons.

(4) Hold in strict confidence those decisions and discussions of the deacon board that call for confidentiality. Insensitivity in this area will destroy the effectiveness of any church board. God's work rightfully demands the greatest care that men can give.

(5) Grow together as brothers in Christ. Serving

on the deacon board will provide the occasion for spiritual growth and development.

The Deacons and the Pastor

The New Testament makes it clear that the primary task of the deacon is to serve. And the pastor, as much as anyone, needs his help. It is to him that he looks for guidance and help in handling the affairs of the congregation.

The entire church will feel the positive effects of a strong and trusting relationship between the pastor and the board of deacons. The harmony that exists in this relationship will soon be copied by the membership of the church.

Several questions should be asked:

(1) Who is the final authority in the local church? Is it the pastor or is it the deacon board? This is hardly a fair question. The Lord is the Head of the church. His is the final authority in the church. Yet he works through men. It is His pleasure that the pastor, in harmony with the deacon board, together seek the will of God for direction in handling the affairs of the church. A spirit of "submitting one to another" should prevail. This is not, however, to lessen the place of the pastor as the under-shepherd over the household of God.

(2) What are the responsibilities of the deacon board to the pastor in matters of finance? The deacon board should be sensitive to the needs of the pastor in this area. An annual review of the pastor's salary and benefits is advisable. The increases in cost of living, the positive performance of the pastor, and a comparable wage analysis should be taken into consideration in setting levels of compensation. A pastor should have faith that the Lord will supply his needs, and the

deacon board should seek the Lord as to their response to his faith. Mutual respect and understanding are imperative on this sensitive issue.

(3) Is it necessary for the deacon board to give gifts to the pastor on special occasions? This will be a matter for individual boards to determine. While a pastor should never expect any kind of "special treatment," there may be occasions when courtesy and love would make the giving of a gift appropriate. There are many ways for a congregation to show their love and appreciation to the pastor, and an occasional gift may be a chosen way to do so. Never should such considerations as these become of major importance, either to the pastor or to the deacon board.

(4) Is it advisable for the deacon board to maintain a retirement program for the pastor? If possible, there should be positive action on this matter. Too often a pastor reaches retirement age and lacks the financial resources to provide for his own welfare. If a pastor has lived in a parsonage during the years of his ministry, he may be without a home at the time of his retirement. A systematic program of investment will eliminate this unfortunate circumstance. Many churches have developed flexible and practical plans for the retirement needs of the pastor.

(5) Is it advisable for the deacon board to grant the pastor leave for study and prayer? Most certainly it is. In addition to vacation time, a pastor should be allowed time away for study and prayer. One pastor is given 2 weeks per year for this purpose. He has commented that during this time he is able to read through a number of books and have time for prayer and meditation. Deacon boards should admonish their pastor to avail himself of this opportunity. The work of God will be blessed by it.

A Staff Manual

In some churches the pastor, in consultation with the deacon board, draws up a manual setting forth the guidelines for the pastor and his staff to eliminate misunderstandings and confusion. The following is a suggested outline for such a manual:

(1) Job descriptions—setting forth the scope of work.

(2) Working hours—giving the daily schedule for office hours.

(3) Hiring procedure—outlining the steps to be followed in filling a vacancy or employing an individual to fill a new position.

(4) Vacation time—stating the number of weeks per year that will be given for vacation.

(5) Sick time, leave of absence, and holidays— giving the guidelines in each of these areas.

(6) Termination—setting forth the responsibilities of the deacon board and the pastor or staff member in this regard.

Each church will want to include additional items in its staff manual in harmony with its distinctive ministry as a church. However, every church, regardless of size, should have specific guidelines in these areas to eliminate misunderstandings and confusion.

A wise pastor will be sure that he and his deacon board have a clear understanding on these practical matters. To set forth guidelines will provide clarification before misunderstanding has occasion to arise.

Calling a Pastor

One of the most awesome responsibilities of the deacon board is to provide continued pastoral ministry in the church. When a pastor resigns, it becomes their responsibility to present to the congregation a nominee or nominees to fill the office of pastor.

Several guidelines will prove helpful in this regard:

(1) Establish procedure. Who will act as the chairman of the board in the absence of a pastor? Will a special committee be chosen to serve as a pulpit committee? Or, will the deacon board act as the pulpit committee? Will the committee visit a prospective pastor's church prior to extending a call? How many services will the prospective pastor conduct before an election is held?

(2) Articulate the qualities of leadership that the church should have at this particular time.

(3) Seek the will of the Lord in leading you to the man who possesses those qualities.

(4) Vote on one man at a time. People become confused when they must choose between men. It is also unfair to a prospective pastor to be subjected to a "competitive" approach to the selection process.

(5) Guide the people to make their choice prayerfully and thoughtfully, rather than on the basis of popularity or personal desire.

(6) Share candidly with the prospective pastor what you as a deacon board feel to be the direction of the church and what you envision for the future.

The choice of a pastor is a most important task. The deacon board that earnestly seeks the Lord and follows a prayerfully developed procedure may be confident that God's man will be chosen to serve them as their spiritual leader.

Questions of a New Pastor

A new pastor will have many questions. These may be asked and answered in a candidate-deacon board meeting prior to the election, or they may be asked and answered after the candidate has been elected as pastor. The timing on this depends on the candidate and the deacon board.

Some questions a new pastor might have are:

(1) Are there any limits on outside ministry?

(2) What is the church's attitude toward the "role of the pastor's wife"? What will her responsibilities be?

(3) What is the procedure for compensation? How are "church-related expenses" handled? Is a parsonage provided? Or, is a housing allowance given?

(4) What is the church's policy on the pastor's participation in sectional, district, and General Council activities?

(5) How would the church feel about the pastor's involvement in an educational program—working on an advanced degree, for example?

There are scores of other questions that need answers when a new pastor arrives, but these are at least indicative. The inclusion of this list of questions is to alert the deacon board to their responsibilities in working closely with a new pastor. It is a time of adjustment for the new pastor as well as for the congregation. Anything the board can do to facilitate that adjustment is time well spent.

Suggestions for Group Study

Self-examination:

(1) Are the deacons' meetings you attend structured for the best utilization of time and to facilitate the decisionmaking process?

(2) Do you have well-defined guidelines for the pastoral staff to follow?

(3) Do you conduct an annual review of all salaries and benefits to be sure they are at the proper levels?

(4) Do you as a deacon have an assigned area of responsibility?

(5) Have you received guidance in fulfilling that responsibility?

(6) Are there opportunities for the deacon board to meet together informally for fellowship and spiritual growth?

Discuss:

(1) Should a deacon be able to succeed himself as a member of the deacon board? If not, why not?

(2) How long should a pastor remain in the same church? What are some of the values of a "long pastorate"?

(3) Who do you feel has the final authority in the church? Do you think this is an unfair question? If so, why?

(4) What are some positive suggestions for creating a worshipful attitude in a deacon board meeting? What place should be given to Bible study and prayer at the regular meetings?

(5) In what ways can deacons help one another to grow spiritually?

(6) What are some ways in which "unity in the board" can be achieved? Is it either possible or advisable to seek unanimity on every issue that is voted upon?

4

THE DEACON
AS A SERVANT

The deacon must have a servant's heart.

Jesus did: "The Son of man came not to be ministered unto, but to minister, and to give his life a ransom for many" (Matthew 20:28).

Paul did: "Though I be free from all men, yet have I made myself servant [doulos—slave] unto all, that I might gain the more" (1 Corinthians 9:19).

And you must, too!

The Servant Principle

What is it that brings satisfaction in the Lord's work? Is it the size of the church in which you work? Is it the honor and prestige of the office you hold? No, satisfaction in the Lord's work is wrapped up in one word—*obedience!*

The slave's greatest delight is to please his master. That is the motivation of his life. He spends himself in service. Through servitude the worker enters the joy of his calling. Obedience becomes the only measure of his success.

Servitude squelches competitiveness and cravings for self-aggrandizement. The servant lives in dependence; his life is dominated by his master. And it is in this that his joy is made complete.

The deacon must live out this principle. His will is

subordinated to the will of Christ. He places the well-being of others above his own. He has an eye for the needs of others. He is dominated by a love and devotion to his Master.

A Demonstration of Servitude

John 13 tells the story.

Jesus, facing the approaching cross, began to wash the feet of the disciples. All was well until He came to Peter: "Never shall You wash my feet!" Jesus said: "If I do not wash you, you have no part with Me." To which Peter replied: "Lord, not my feet only, but also my hands and my head" (vv. 8, 9, NASB).

Then, at the end of the story, we read: "A slave is not greater than his master; neither one who is sent greater than the one who sent him" (v. 16, NASB).

The message is clear: "You also ought to wash one another's feet." The call is to service!

Ministry Through Ushering

First impressions are most important. How people are made to feel between the parking lot and the pew will directly affect their attitude toward the church and their ability to freely worship the Lord.

If parking is a problem, was there anyone there to assist?

Was there anyone at the door to offer a friendly smile and word of welcome?

Was the church clean, tidy, and properly climatized?

Was there someone there to assist them in locating a comfortable seat in the sanctuary?

Did anyone offer assistance when they noticed the presence of a small child?

People must "feel good" about the way in which

they are treated. It is the responsibility of leadership to be sure that coming to church is a pleasant experience for the worshiper.

What are the practical principles for effective ushering?

(1) Ushering is a ministry unto the Lord. This is the first step. The men who accept a position on the ushering staff must feel in their hearts that their service is unto the Lord. The acceptance of this principle will produce diligence and devotion. There is no greater service than service to the Lord. The usher is called of God. His work is the discharging of a divine commission.

(2) Treat the worshiper as a welcome guest. Why is it that invited guests are given such careful consideration in homes, but sometimes such careless treatment in church? A successful pastor challenged a group of ministers: "If 100 new people came to your church next Sunday morning, would you be prepared to receive them?"

The point is well taken. Too often people are "unattended" as they "shift for themselves" in getting ready for the worship service. "Where is the nursery? Where are the rest rooms? Can I find a seat in the back? What time does the service begin?" And there is no one available to anticipate the questions and be ready with the answers. It is no wonder that some churches attract few new members from the community. They have not learned to treat the worshiper as a welcome guest.

(3) Organize. Here is a checklist:

(a) Has a head usher been appointed to coordinate the ushering program?

(b) Does the head usher meet regularly

with the pastor to coordinate the ushering program with him?

(c) Are the ushers provided with a schedule to indicate when they are to serve?

(d) Is there a training program in which the "mechanics" of ushering are taught (e.g., seating people, receiving the offering, passing out bulletins)?

(e) Is each usher prepared to give answers to the questions the worshiper may ask?

(4) Look the part. A dress code is in order. Ushers represent the ministry of the church, and they should look the part. Most men have at least one suit, and that is what they should wear when they are on duty as ushers.

Some may object: "Why do we need to give so much attention to externals? It smacks of a kind of formality—maybe it's best to just 'freewheel.' "

The justification for a sharp, well-organized ushering program is clear. The worshiper must be freed from concerns that ought not to be his so he may be free to worship the Lord. To do this is the usher's ministry.

In most churches, the deacons lead the way as a vital part of the ushering ministry.

Ministry Through the Communion Service

The Communion service is an essential part of the church's spiritual life. It is that time when the body of Christ meets to celebrate the death, resurrection, and second coming of Jesus Christ. The deacon board will want to do its part to make that service what the Lord intended it to be.

Each pastor has his own chosen way of serving the emblems and conducting the Communion service. He will instruct the deacon board, and any others who may assist, in what he wants them to do to be sure the service flows smoothly and without needless interruption.

Just a few observations on the Communion service:

(1) Make the proper arrangements. Be sure that someone prepares the emblems ahead of time and that the Communion table is attractively arranged. The trays should be polished, the table dusted, and the covering cloth clean.

(2) Avoid routine. Let there be a flexibility as the Holy Spirit directs. Prayer for the sick can be a part of the Communion service. It may be fitting for a member to speak of the significance of the Communion service to him personally. There are many possibilities for variation. Remember, too, that the Communion service may be held at any time when the church is together. Variety here may be good as well.

(3) Know its significance. In the Communion service the body of Christ meets in celebration and fellowship. It is a time of rejoicing over the victory of the Cross and the blessed hope of the believer. It is also a time for the members of the body of Christ to renew their commitment to one another. Paul instructs the church: "For he who eats and drinks, eats and drinks judgment to himself, if he does not judge the body rightly" (1 Corinthians 11:29, NASB). The Lord's body is not only the body of Jesus but now His body, the Church. The Communion service draws the members of the church together in love and devotion, first to Christ and then to one another.

Ministry Through Visitation

Deacons are called to serve. Part of that service will involve visitation. The dedicated deacon will not shrink from that responsibility.

51

There are some rules deacons should follow in visiting the members of the church they serve:

(1) The visitation ministry of the deacon should be coordinated with the pastor. Since the total care of the congregation is the concern of the pastor, he should be advised of the deacon's efforts in visitation. His guidance will be of great value to the deacon.

(2) The deacon should be careful that his calls are well-timed and appropriate. People resent being bothered at meal time, unannounced visits, or any contact that may be considered an interruption. A phone call will pave the way for a well-timed visit.

(3) Lengthy visits are not usually advisable. Most people have demanding schedules and will appreciate the deacon's respect for their time.

(4) Whenever possible, a deacon should take his wife with him when making calls. Or, he may wish to ask one of the other deacons to accompany him. Going "two by two" has many benefits and will eliminate potentially uncomfortable situations.

(5) Deacons should be positive, supportive, and prayerful. They should refrain from involving themselves in conversations that will put others in a bad light or in any way create a negative impression of the church and its leadership.

The deacon may be summoned to a home to pray for a member who is ill, to counsel with a member about difficulties in the home, to explain to a member the various opportunities for ministry in the church, or just to encourage a member by showing a personal interest in his spiritual growth and development.

The deacon will also be asked to call on members who have been hospitalized. The principles noted above are applicable for hospital calls as well. However, just a couple of further suggestions:

(1) Plan to visit the patient during normal visiting hours. When possible, refrain from asking for special visitation privileges.

(2) Keep the visit cheerful, positive, and brief. Remember, the patient may not feel well enough to enjoy a lengthy visit. A 5-minute visit is usually adequate. Obviously, there are exceptions.

(3) Avoid speaking to the patient about the details of his illness. That is the doctor's responsibility.

(4) Close the visit with prayer. Believe that God is acting as you agree together for healing and encouragement.

Ministry Through Counseling

The deacon is often called upon to fill the role of a counselor. His counsel may be sought at the altar as he prays with a member, during a house call, or at a chance meeting on any number of occasions. He will be asked to give advice in a variety of areas: domestic problems, church problems, spiritual problems, health problems, vocational problems, financial problems—just to mention a few.

Some deacons are well qualified to meet the challenge of counseling. Others feel ill-at-ease and unsure of themselves as they attempt to fill this role. The following guidelines will be of value in helping the deacon understand some of the basics in this vital area of ministry to the church:

(1) Learn to distinguish between the counseling a deacon should accept and that which belongs to the pastor. Do not hesitate to say, "I believe you should seek direction from the pastor on this problem." Most people will readily understand.

(2) Remember that "being a good listener" is a fundamental principle in effective counseling. A

deacon does not need to be highly skilled to listen with his mind and heart to the needs of a member in the church.

(3) Hold the affairs of the membership in confidence. People with problems seek those counselors who will refrain from sharing personal information with others.

(4) Develop an objectivity in your counseling ministry. Do not get emotionally involved or press the counselee to share information that may be inappropriate. Great sensitivity in this area is demanded.

(5) Understand that the Holy Spirit will guide you in your counseling ministry. He is the Spirit of truth. His enablement is available to all who earnestly seek it with a humble heart.

A deacon's ministry as a counselor can be most beneficial to the church if it is conducted with a deep sense of propriety. It is an area of vulnerability and ready pitfalls. The wise deacon will share with the pastor his progress and problems as a counselor. The pastor's encouragement and guidance will help the deacon make the most of this valuable opportunity.

Ministry to New Members

In many churches the pastor presents a list of candidates for membership to the deacon board for their review and acceptance. The candidate is then presented to the church and given the right hand of fellowship. Sometimes this is all that happens—and the new member is left to discover on his own what it means to be a member of the church.

The deacons can be of great assistance to the pastor in the process of bringing new people into the full membership of the church:

(1) A training class for prospective members

should be conducted by the pastor and attended by the deacons. The class may be held for several Sunday evenings just prior to the evening service. Or, it may be scheduled for any other time that is mutually convenient. The class should deal with doctrine, membership requirements, faithfulness in attendance, financial support, service opportunities, and church structure and practice.

(2) The list of candidates should be divided among the members of the deacon board and each candidate personally contacted to be sure that a wise decision can be made as to their acceptability for membership. This also has the advantage of giving the candidate a sense of belonging and a feeling that the church cares and takes membership seriously.

(3) In some churches a special banquet is planned for deacons, pastors, and new members. This practice will place emphasis on the importance of church membership.

(4) New members should be encouraged to find a place of ministry in the church. Some method should be devised to assess abilities and calling. A recommendation can be made as to an appropriate area of ministry. However, it is not always wise to "push" new members into responsibilities. They may need time to grow in the fellowship of the church before they are "tied down" to specific tasks.

Good church members are not the product of chance. They are produced through the work of the Holy Spirit and careful and prayerful instruction and guidance. One of the many joys of being in spiritual leadership is to watch the members of the body of Christ grow into maturity and useful service for Christ. Deacons are key men in that process.

Ministry Through Discipline

The pattern for church discipline is set forth in Matthew 18:15-17. The pattern contains the following provisions:

(1) The offended brother goes to the brother who has offended him and speaks correctively to him about his sin. If the brother who has been guilty of offense receives the correction, the matter is closed.

(2) When the offending brother refuses correction, the offended brother returns to him the second time with a witness.

(3) If the offending brother refuses "joint correction," the matter then goes to the entire church for their disposition.

The Early Church understood the importance of church discipline. Ananias and Sapphira were found guilty of misrepresentation and thievery. Peter pronounced the judgment of God upon them (Acts 5:1-11). The New Testament is evidence that the Early Church practiced discipline in the care of its members. The apostle Paul instructed the leadership of the Corinthian church to expel from its membership a man who was conducting himself in an immoral way.

Unfortunately, the church today has often lost sight of the positive impact of properly executed discipline. Its members are sometimes left unchecked in their questionable conduct. The church, by virtue of its neglect, contributes to the perpetration of sin in its membership and stands by to watch itself being stripped of its authority and power. Great fear came upon the Early Church as a consequence of its disciplining action. Would not the same thing be true in the church today?

There are cautions and guidance that must be noted:

(1) Pray for guidance. The Biblical pattern is workable only in a spiritual context.

(2) Act in unity and peace. If there is division among the deacons, nothing should be done until prayer has resolved the disunity.

(3) Be redemptive in attitude. Paul's rather harsh treatment of the man in Corinth was intended to bring him to truth and repentance. Evidence in the Scriptures would suggest that he was in time restored to fellowship. Discipline must never be vindictive and destructive. The goal is always redemptive.

(4) Be quick to forgive. The Spirit of Jesus was one of forgiveness. He forgave before there was any indication of repentance. So must we—in our hearts! Forgiveness, true forgiveness, means that we not only pardon the offender but we forget the offense. The deacon must have grace enough to do this.

Ministry by Example

The next chapter will deal with the deacon as a person. But it should be noted here that the strength of a deacon's ministry, in any of the areas discussed above, is largely dependent on the qualities of godliness that he demonstrates. People learn best by looking at models. They do not hear with their ears nearly so effectively as they hear with their eyes. The deacon lives in a glass house. He is watched by the church and by the world.

It is just at this point that he has an opportunity to be a powerful influence for the Lord. People are watching. That is good. Now they will see for themselves the power of God at work in a man's life.

Suggestions for Group Study

Introspection: It is time to evaluate the areas of

ministry discussed in this chapter as they are presently being conducted in your church. What are the areas of strengths and weaknesses? What are the underlying reasons for these apparent weaknesses and strengths? What positive suggestions can be offered to strengthen the ministry of the church in each of these areas?

Discuss:

(1) What prompts deacons to resist the "servant role" to which they are called? Do they feel personally threatened by the thought of being a servant? Could it be an ego problem?

(2) Why is it that some people are particular about the details of their personal lives but are indifferent about the details that affect the program of the church?

(3) Why is it important that the pastor and each deacon with whom he works maintain a positive and open relationship?

(4) Do you agree that a deacon lives in a glass house? If so, in what sense? In light of this, what kind of life should he live?

5

THE DEACON
AS A PERSON

The deacon has been stereotyped. Somehow he comes out as someone not quite human. He has succumbed to a process of depersonalization and is hardly himself.

This ought not to be. A deacon is first a person—created like everyone else in the image of God. Then he is a man of God—dedicated to Jesus Christ as Lord and Saviour. And, last, he is a servant of Christ to carry on His work on this earth.

He fits no mold, puts on no airs, and creates no images. He is simply a man called of God to minister to the church. He dares to be human, he fits in, he enjoys living, and he is a regular guy. Away with all stereotyped notions of what a deacon must appear to be. That does not count. He is first and always God's man doing what God wants him to do. And that is enough—he can do nothing else.

This chapter is designed to explode that notion; to show that a deacon makes a mark for God by being a person, a whole person, God's person.

The Deacon's Commitment

There is a high cost for leadership.

Paul says that Jesus "made himself of no reputation" (Philippians 2:7). That, in summary, is the cost of leadership. A spiritual leader must make himself of no reputation, and that calls for commitment.

There are some questions that a prospective deacon should ask himself before allowing his name to be placed in nomination:

(1) Can I place God's work above my own work?

(2) Can I put truth above personal popularity?

(3) Can I accept accusations without demanding personal justification?

(4) Can I absorb criticism without passing it on to others?

(5) Can I hear gossip and not speak it to others?

(6) Can I stand up for right although it puts me in the minority?

The deacon must consider the cost of leadership before he accepts the call. The call demands a high level of personal and spiritual commitment.

The Deacon's Devotional Life

The Scriptures set forth a principle that will sustain the deacon in the most difficult and trying circumstances: "Greater is he that is in [us], than he that is in the world" (1 John 4:4).

This means that the Lord has put within us a flow of power that is greater than the resistance of this world. What a promise for the spiritual leader! When the inner resource is strong, the challenge of ministry can never be too heavy.

I often tell myself, "Keep the inner flow strong!" That is the key. If a spiritual leader is strong in spirit, he can face with courage any obstacle that may come his way. In this section of the manual that principle becomes the focus.

How can a deacon see this inner resource developed? How can his spirit be strong in the power of

Christ? How can he maintain his perspective and his sense of priority amid the rush of living and serving? The answer is found in his devotional life.

Here are suggestions that may be of help:

(1) Live in the presence of Christ. There is no division between secular things and spiritual things in the life of a disciple. The deacon does not pass in and out of the presence of Christ, nor does he divide his church life from his daily life. He lives in the presence of Christ and views his entire life as a ministry unto God and man. His recreation, study, prayer, and meditations are viewed as one—it is all done as unto the Lord. It is part of that "balanced view" that spiritual leaders must understand and practice. One activity is never "more spiritual" than another activity if both are fulfilled in the will of God.

(2) Take time to be alone. "Treadmill living" does not build spiritual character. A man of God must have time to be quiet and alone. Being alone in meditation and prayer refurbishes the spirit and sparks a new love for God and His work. It is the time to "get it all together," to reflect, evaluate, ponder, dream, and expect—and it must be done alone.

This time should include supplication, intercession, and prayer. But it also should include time to listen, to be quiet before God, to look within, and to enjoy God. It might be called the "act of silence" or simply "learning to be still." In any case, it is a key to spiritual power and effective service.

(3) Love the Word. Men grounded in the Scriptures are stable and strong. Their faith and service has found a footing. They are unmovable and their lives have order and purpose. They have tapped a source of power that is renewable day by day.

As a practical suggestion for Bible reading, some

have found it helpful to read passages from various parts of the Bible, in contrast to a "through-the-Bible" approach that runs from Genesis through to Revelation. A passage from the historical books, the poetical books, the prophets, the Gospels, and the Epistles would give a balance to Biblical studies that could be both interesting and helpful. Of course, this is a personal matter. The important thing is that the Bible be the "big Book" in the deacon's life.

(4) Experience the dynamic of prayer. Here is a mighty resource. Prayer knows no locked gates nor resistance to distance. It has no fear in the face of unbelief and dares to return time and time again. It is limitless in its power.

A visiting teacher shared the following outline for intercessory prayer. You may find it to be a guide to a new dimension of prayer:

(a) Pray for those in leadership throughout the world.

(b) Pray for spiritual leaders directly over you.

(c) Pray for the city in which God has placed you.

(d) Pray for your nation.

(e) Pray for the fellowship to which God has called you.

(f) Pray for your immediate family.

(g) Pray for lost souls that God brings across your path.

(h) Pray for new converts and needy Christians.

(i) Pray for neighbors on your street.

(j) Pray for those who speak against you or persecute you.

(k) Pray for nations almost entirely unreached with the gospel.

(l) Pray for those who are Communists, Buddhists, Hinduists, Shintoists, and Muslims.

(m) Pray for brothers and sisters in Christ who are without religious freedom.

(n) Pray that our vision and borders may be enlarged.

(o) Pray for all the nations of the world.

Intercessory prayer has a worldwide impact. It knows no language or ethnic barriers. All it needs is a humble heart from which it may rise.

(5) Be a priest in your home. The deacon's first call is to his family. He must be a spiritual leader in his own home before he can hope to be a leader in the church. It is fitting to speak of the exercise of his priestly ministry to his family as a part of his devotional life.

A regular family altar is a must. There is no substitute for it. A deacon who fails to pray with his family and read the Bible with them is guilty of the most serious kind of neglect. Time must be taken for this.

Here are some guidelines for family worship:

(a) Involve every member of the family in some way. Even small children can contribute with a consenting smile or a clap of their hands.

(b) Relate the worship time to daily living. What does the passage say to us in a practical way? How will its truths change our lives? What effect will our prayer time have on our lives?

(c) Believe that Christ is at work. It is your place to stir faith in the hearts of your children. They must see that Christ is alive; that prayer does change things. Your attitude will prompt faith. You hold the key!

The Deacon's Wife

Your wife will share your call and ministry as a deacon if you will give her the chance. Do you know that she wants to feel that your ministry is hers, that your burden is hers, that your heartaches are hers, and that your rejoicings are hers? She wants to be involved—and she will be if you will give her an opportunity.

"Wow, will I ever be glad when he gets off the deacon board!" It is your fault, sir. You have given her cause to be negative. You have ignored the contribution she could have made, and you have given her cause for distrust by your indifferent and critical spirit.

Here are some tips for deacons' wives:

(1) Be supportive. There will be times when your friendly smile and word of encouragement will help your husband over a difficult and trying time.

(2) Be confidential. The matters discussed in a meeting of the deacon board are confidential. You will hurt the work of God by sharing information that is not yours to share.

(3) Be helpful. Your husband will need your counsel on many matters that pertain to his work as a deacon. He needs to feel he can share matters with you, seek your counsel, hear your suggestions, and still know that those confidences will be kept. You are a valuable resource for your husband's ministry as a deacon.

(4) Be forgiving. You may feel resentful toward those who unjustly criticize the decisions of the deacon board, and a root of bitterness can begin to grow in your heart. This must not be allowed to happen. Learn to forgive and forget. Remember, bitterness will hurt you first—and then the work of God.

A deacon's wife is a valuable asset to the work of God and should not be taken for granted or ignored. She has much to offer. Her sensitivity and perceptiveness can be a great blessing to her husband as he carries on his work as a deacon.

The Deacon's Children

The measure of a man is his children! You can tell a great deal about a father by watching his children. They are a reflection of his character and conduct.

Is it any wonder that the apostle Paul states emphatically that no man should attempt to rule the household of God until he first shows that he is able to rule his own house well? It is easily understood why Paul admonished spiritual leaders to keep their children in submission. Children are a credit or a liability to the ministry of any man.

But let's look at it from the children's side of things:

"Don't do that . . . your father is a deacon in the church!"

"He sure doesn't act like a deacon's kid to me!"

"Oh, well, what can you expect from a deacon's kids!"

Is it any wonder that the children of deacons sometimes resent the "special place" assigned to them? Is it too much to expect that the members of the church hold a consistent standard of conduct for all the children? It is tragic to single out any children and make demands upon them that are inconsistent with the standards for the entire group. Fairness is a must.

However, the children of a deacon should be very grateful that their father is a deacon. They are often privileged to meet interesting spiritual leaders who come to their home. They are sometimes included in gatherings of Christian people because their father is a deacon. And the blessing of having a godly father, one who is qualified to serve as a deacon, is of no small consideration.

A wise deacon will take time to be with his children. He will play with them, do things with them, and develop a relationship of trust and love with them. There is no substitute for just being together and doing things together. The church is blessed by spiritual leaders who are part of a vibrant and spiritual family unit.

David was one of Israel's most dynamic leaders. He was a man after God's own heart. But he failed as a father.

It is possible that Absalom was raised by the servants in the palace, since David was too busy writing psalms and administering a nation to spend time with his son. There was possibly no time for a loving relationship to develop between David and Absalom.

At the news of Absalom's death, David cried out: "Oh my son Absalom! My son, my son Absalom! would God I had died for thee" (2 Samuel 18:33).

It did not have to be. Though David was a spiritual giant, he failed in the most important area of life. He left to others a task that only he could do.

The warning is clear, and every deacon needs to reflect on this story. It shows the awful consequences of confused priorities and inverted values. Children come first, for they are a sacred trust.

Here is the order of things:
   (a) God, first
   (b) Wife, second
   (c) Children, third
   (d) Church, fourth

If you live by this order, God will be honored through your family and you will multiply your ministry through them.

The Deacon's Reputation

You have heard it said: "And he claims to be a deacon in the church!" Unfortunately, his reputation does not complement his office or his testimony as a Christian.

All that you are either complements the work of the Lord or it detracts from it. You live in a glass house, and people are watching you.

They want to see a faith that matters all week long and that is evidenced by a transformed life. They want to see Christ in you! When you said, "I accept the office to which I have been elected," you placed on yourself this responsibility.

Is your house in good repair?
Do you dress as neatly as possible?
Do you take time to wash your car?
Is your lawn neatly trimmed?
Do you pay your bills on time?

Yes, these things really do matter. People rightfully expect something more from you. They will expect that your house complement the neighborhood and that you dress properly. They will expect that your word is as good as your signature. It is all a part of the office you hold.

The Deacon's Personality

The deacon's work is with people, and he must be able to get along well with them.

One minister has said, "People must like you before you can minister to them." To an extent, that is true.

67

At least, they must have a respect for you if they are to receive your ministry.

The prophets were despised, but they were honored and respected. This is the key. You are not in a popularity contest, but people must hold you in honor if they are to receive spiritual ministry from you. So, in a practical sense, your personality is vital to your effectiveness as a servant of the Lord.

Listed here are some principles for working with people that will help the deacon in his ministry:

(1) Maintain a servant's posture. Over and over this has been stated. But it is essential. The people you serve will follow your guidance if they sense that you have a high regard for their needs and are determined to help them in any way you can. Humility is a vital attribute in the deacon's life.

(2) Be positive. Any of us can walk into a committee meeting and greatly influence the atmosphere of the meeting just by our attitude. Don't say, "My, we have some terrible problems. I doubt if we're going to be successful. Maybe we should think of giving up on this project. I'm losing heart."

Be assured the suggestion will cut like a knife of destruction.

Instead, be positive: "Isn't it great to be in God's work! When we face the inevitable problems, God always has a solution for us. Isn't it wonderful to know that out of this meeting is going to come a plan for fulfilling the mission to which God has called us!"

People gravitate toward positive people. They respond with joy and dedication if someone will just lead the way.

Remember, God is positive. He is bringing the world to a glorious consummation. He has the direction of history before Him and the last chapter is one of victory. Those who serve Him and work for the building of His kingdom must possess this attribute. Be positive, and view every problem as an opportunity.

(3) Keep the goal in mind. Someone has said: "He wins battles but loses wars." Have you seen this happening? I am sure you have—people who challenge every issue and drive it into the ground. With pride they say, "I won that round." But, unfortunately, people resist their leadership and they never fulfill their potential.

Always keep your eyes on the long-range goal. Don't make little issues a matter of life and death. Develop a plan and have a long-range program. Learn to give a little here and there to see the goal reached, assuming the compromise does not involve principle. You can prove you are right on a point, but if a person goes away insulted you have lost a friend.

(4) Be yourself. Don't "act like a deacon," however some people think one is to act. Just be God's man—yourself—free, relaxed, and confident in His grace. People will love you for it.

Don't forget, God has made you. Be pleased with His work and have confidence in yourself. Know that you can just be yourself and please God.

God's glory is best reflected in the lives of men who are confident of their standing in Christ; who know that all God wants is obedience and that the life of simple trust is enough to fulfill His plan.

(5) Respect others. People will often disagree with you. There will be people whom you find it hard to appreciate. Yet, you must respect them and value their opinions and observations. They are also mem-

bers of the body of Christ. Paul says that the parts of the Body that seem to be weak are indispensable, and that the Lord has tempered the Body together to form the composite that pleases Him. It is your privilege to serve the whole Body. Every member is important to God, and to you, too.

(6) Don't retaliate. There will be plenty of times when you will wish to "fight back," but you cannot—for God has called you to be a leader. The Lord is your defense, and you need not feel that every accusation must be answered and every deed justified. It is the Lord's work. You represent Him. If your heart is right, He will vindicate you and the truth will march on.

You will be pleased at the response you will receive from most people if you are kind, loving, and willing to listen. Usually all that people need is information and someone who is willing to listen. If you will maintain a spirit of respect and openness, the Holy Spirit will use you as a catalyst to maintain unity in the church you serve.

The Deacon's Reward

There is no higher joy than service. Jesus, for the joy that was set before Him, endured the cross. His meat was to do the will of the Father. On the cross, when Jesus said: "It is finished," all of heaven and earth was made to rejoice.

The deacon's reward is simply this: the realized joy of service. He seeks no applause, trophies, or acclaim, but is satisfied just to know that he has been able to serve the people of God in love.

What is your motive in being a deacon? Are you bent on making a name for yourself? Is it your goal to "put your mark" on the work of God so you will be applauded by men? Or, do you fulfill your call for the sheer joy of knowing you are entering into Christ's will for your life?

The Scriptures warn us that we should not become "weary in well doing." Some Christians work and toil, give and strive, until in time they become exhausted and discouraged. This ought not to be. A pastor should sense this before it goes this far and put a stop to it. A deacon must not allow himself to come to this place. He must keep the joy of service before him at all times. By living in the awareness that all his efforts are for Christ and for the building of His kingdom, he will not fall prey to this temptation.

Only eternity is going to show clearly the reward of the faithful deacon and the measure of his ministry. The Lord has set the deacon in His church to carry on His work. Just to know that ought to be enough!

Suggestions for Group Study

Personal Projects:

(1) Analyze your own personality. What do you see to be strengths and weaknesses? In your judgment, how do you get along with people? What can you do to make your relationships with others more constructive?

(2) Consider each area of ministry outlined in this chapter and think through your personal adaptability to it. What can you do to be better prepared to serve in each area?

(3) Evaluate the strengths and weaknesses in your relationship with your family. Is your family growing spiritually? Are you doing your part to

lead the family in worship and prayer? Is the Bible
an important book in your home?

Discuss:

(1) Why is the deacon's wife so important to his
ministry?

(2) Do you think that it is important that a
deacon dress well, drive a clean car, and keep his
lawn trimmed? If so, why?

(3) Why do you think a deacon's devotional
life is important?

6

THE DEACON
AS A PROBLEM SOLVER

It's time now to apply the principles outlined in the previous chapters.

The problems raised in this chapter are typical of the complex and difficult matters that come to deacons for solution. The life situations cited here, while typical, are purely hypothetical. This chapter is intended only as a learning experience. It is important to remember that the pastor should be aware of any official action taken on matters such as the ones given here.

(1) Suppose a deacon learns from reliable sources that a member of the congregation is involved in a financial scheme that is both dishonest and illegal. The member has been in the church for many years and has held places of responsibility in the past. He has a lovely family and is faithful to the church in attendance and support. What should the informed deacon do?

Alternative Actions:

—Take the matter to the deacon board for corrective action.

—Go to his wife and ask her to talk with her husband about his questionable conduct.

—Ask several of the key members their opinion about the matter.

—Just pray about it and do nothing.

—Take the matter lightly and share it with others as a point of conversation.

—Go to the pastor and let him decide what to do.

—Never tell anyone but use your influence to keep him out of places of responsibility in the church.

Suggested Approach:

Matthew 18:15-17 provides the necessary guidelines. Go to the brother, no one else, and confront him with the matter. Deal with him in love and firmness. Be objective. Check your information to be sure it is correct. If he repents, the matter is closed. If not, follow the two additional steps outlined in Matthew 18.

After he has repented, you should counsel him to share this area of difficulty with his wife (if appropriate) and with the pastor. Both are entitled to this information, but it should come from him and not you.

Now, go back over the alternative actions and follow their effects. You will quickly discover that the Biblical solution keeps the problem in perspective, does not hurt other people unnecessarily, is redemptive in its thrust, avoids gossip and false accusations, keeps the problem as small as possible, and does not hurt the church.

(2) Suppose there is a growing awareness in the membership that the Sunday school superin-

tendent should be replaced. The superintendent has served the church for years in an effective way. Likely he has simply grown weary with the responsibility and has ceased to be effective. Yet, he has not indicated his willingness to step aside. His 2-year term will not expire for another 18 months. What action should be taken?

Alternative Actions:

—Wait it out . . . and at the end of his term vote someone else in to take his place.

—Discuss the matter freely among the members and hope that someone will leak the information that he is no longer wanted, and in that way force his resignation.

—Encourage, in subtle ways, a "cool" attitude toward the superintendent, hoping he will sense something is wrong and retire.

—Complain to the pastor until he is forced to replace him with someone more qualified.

—Commit the matter to the Lord and do nothing.

—Refuse to cooperate with any programs that originate with him.

Suggested Approach:

The apostle Paul was forthright in his dealings with the church. He placed high value on truthfulness and openness and did not hesitate to give pointed admonitions to the leaders of the churches. He put the work of God above personalities.

The deacons and the pastor should weigh the matter, holding it before the Lord in prayer. Is it really true that this brother is as ineffective as it seems? Could he be challenged to approach his work with the zeal he once knew? Is there something bothering him that could easily be corrected if known? Or, must he be replaced?

The deacons and the pastor, after prayer, should act. To do nothing is only to perpetuate the problem. If the superintendent must be replaced, it should be done with love and openness. On the other hand, if he can be helped to regain his previous effectiveness, that becomes a viable option. In any event, the board must be ready to act. If they do so in love, they can be confident that their decision will have a positive impact.

Now, go over the alternatives noted above and follow their possible effects. It is apparent that distrust, fear, pride, deception, and ignorance surround each in one way or another. Yet, such alternatives are sometimes followed and with them come the sad effects of poor leadership decisions.

(3) Suppose the pastor has brought upon himself the sharp criticism of many members of the church. His words are sometimes curt, he lacks sensitivity to the feelings of people, and he sometimes acts impulsively. In one way or another, he manages to alienate people from him. He is a good preacher and in many ways is an excellent pastor.

Alternative Actions:

—Encourage complaining members to be patient and "wait it out."

—Cut the pastor's salary and hope he gets the hint and resigns.

—Be uncooperative and cool and anticipate that he will either change or quit.

—Discuss the problem openly with other members to see if the negative feeling is widespread.

—Call a special meeting and force a resignation.

—Pray but take no action.

Suggested Approach:

The Scriptures are clear: we are both to pray for those who have the spiritual leadership over us, and to show high honor to those who are ministers for Christ. However, this in no way precludes the action of the deacon board to deal with a very real problem. In this case, something must be done.

The deacon board should prayerfully discuss the problem with the pastor. He should be confronted with the reports that have come from the members. In some instances it will be clear that supportive facts are missing, so these reports should be discounted. In a spirit of openness, the facts will emerge.

With correction must come the extension of forgiveness and restoration. The deacon board offers love and prayers. The situation can be cleared up and the work can go on. This is the ministry of the Holy Spirit to the body of Christ through its leadership.

Many ministries will be preserved if deacons will accept their responsibilities in ministering to the needs of their pastor. Their love and support will help him to be the man that God wants him to be.

If you follow any of the alternatives noted above, you will readily see their folly. Yet, these alternatives are often pursued. Churches are hurt, pastors discouraged, and the work of building the Kingdom seriously impaired.

(4) Suppose the church is in the midst of a building program. Although both the pastor and the deacon board had felt satisfied that all construction costs were accurately projected, such was not the case. With the building 80 percent completed, the funds were depleted and construction ceased. The congregation began looking for explanations. The pastor and the deacon board felt defensive. A wedge was driven between leadership and the people. Something had to be done.

Alternative Actions:

—Continue the search for the people responsible for the incorrect cost estimates, and lay the blame at their feet.

—Call for new leadership. Ask for the resignation of the pastor and the deacon board.

—Discuss with others the irresponsibility of leadership and rally support for faultfinding.

—Pray but do nothing more.

Suggested Approach:

Leadership must be accountable. The deacon board should assess its position. Why did the situation develop as it did? Who is responsible for the error? Was it clearly inadvertent and accidental?

A report should be made to the congregation by the deacon board. The report should be informative but not vindictive or faultfinding.

A positive solution should be offered to meet the problem. The entire congregation should be encouraged to rise to the occasion and believe God for an answer. A great problem can be turned into a great victory.

People respond to a challenge. With guidance, they will work together to see the project completed. The Holy Spirit has anointed leadership to rise to the occasion and bring forth a program that will lead to success.

Deacons who are nondefensive, filled with faith, ready to admit error, and prayerful will find a way to solve the most difficult problems. If you analyze the "alternative solutions" noted above, you will see they are well-worn but harmful to the work of God. They are in violation of the principles of leadership that have been outlined in this manual.

(5) Suppose a neighboring assembly attracts to it some of the members of the congregation. A feeling of unrest fills the vacuum created by their departure. Rumors begin about why people are leaving and what is wrong with the church. The deacon board is in a quandry as to what should be done. There is fear that the exodus may continue.

Alternative Actions:

—Blame the pastor for failing to hold the people.

—Share in the discussion about "what's wrong with the church."

—Become embittered toward those who have left.

—Resent the pastor in the neighboring church.

—Try to discourage others from leaving by speaking ill of the people in the other church.

Suggested Approach:

Any church will experience this situation from

time to time. Granted, it is time for the deacon board and pastor to evaluate the ministry of the church, but it is not the occasion for panic. People do change churches for a variety of reasons. Their leaving does not necessarily indicate any failure in the church they have been attending.

Unless there have been areas of difficulty, people who leave should go with the blessing of the pastor and board. It is unwise to use any kind of force or coercion to get people to stay. If they feel it is time for them to leave, it is best to comply with their wishes.

Above all, be sure that no bitterness or jealousy is allowed to creep in. Speak well of other churches. Rejoice in their progress. Be supportive of what they are doing for Christ. It is all the Lord's work, and that is the compelling principle of all service.

Resentments sometimes follow a member who leaves to attend another assembly. This must not be. Everyone suffers when this is allowed to take place. A spirit of love and understanding must govern these matters.

Satan uses every negative occasion to further his cause, but the church must not fall prey. Rejoice over the work of God in every place, for it is the Lord's work and He will build His church.

(6) Suppose a doctrinal controversy has developed in the church. Certain members have been influenced to follow the advocates of a "new truth." At this point only a few members of the church are involved, but their influence is strong. The pastor and deacon board are united that something must be done.

Alternative Actions:

—Do nothing. Assume that the problem will disappear with the passing of time.

—Start a hostility crusade against the group that has apparently moved away from sound doctrine.

—Send each member who is involved a letter of disfellowship.

—Announce to the church that anyone involved in doctrinal controversy will be disciplined immediately.

—Call in the district officials to deal with the problem.

Suggested Approach:

It is the charge of the pastor and deacon board to preserve the tenets of faith to which the church subscribes. When members break from that position, the matter must be dealt with.

Some questions:

(a) What is the exact nature of the so-called "departure from faith"? Is the departure real or fabricated?

(b) Are those involved actually committed to this "new doctrine," or are they only inquirers?

(c) Is the doctrinal issue of consequence or is it incidental to the general development of doctrine in the Bible?

(d) Are the members involved militant and zealous in their approach to their "new doctrinal insight"? Are they influencing other members?

(e) Is this doctrinal departure in direct conflict with the tenets of faith to which the church subscribes, or is it but a matter of interpretation?

Answers to these questions should be sought from the people whose conduct and beliefs are being questioned. A serious attempt should be made to understand exactly what they do believe and whether, in fact, there is a clear indication that wrong doctrine is involved.

Many times a "doctrinal difficulty" can be removed by a clear definition of terms. People may appear to have views quite different from ours, yet the differences evaporate when the issues are clearly articulated.

Be patient! Give people an opportunity to reevaluate. Perhaps they are momentarily impressed with some "new teaching" but will hold it only briefly. A wise pastor and deacon board will move cautiously and prayerfully in matters such as this.

However, if members can no longer subscribe to the basic tenets of faith which the church holds, it would be well for them to choose another fellowship. The pastor and deacon board should insist that their departure be in a context of love. It is wrong for animosity and bitterness to creep into situations like this. They need not!

What are the principles that lead to effective problem solving?

(1) Seek the will of God. A deacon who makes this a priority will find that he is effective as a problem solver. The Lord has given to the deacon a discerning spirit and an understanding heart. If he uses these resources he will know the power of Christ and find that he is able to deal effectively with the areas of difficulty that arise.

"Lord, what would you have me to do?"
"Lord, let the Spirit of truth prevail."
"Lord, open my heart to your ways."
"Lord, give me your solution to this problem."

(2) Be objective. A wise deacon will not allow himself to be caught in the emotions of the problems with which he works. He must pursue truth and retain his sense of objectivity. As a leader he does not have the option of "speaking his mind" and "having the last word." His mission is greater than winning an argument and establishing his own point of view.

A deacon who allows himself to become emotionally involved in the problems he faces will be unable to see the alternatives clearly. He will act more from feeling than from fact. Objectivity is a must in the problem-solving process.

(3) Take people seriously. There is equality in the body of Christ. Every member is important. And it is the responsibility of leadership to take seriously the needs of each member.

Mutual respect goes a long way in solving problems and meeting the needs of members. If a member understands that there is a true concern for his area of difficulty, he will be helped and encouraged. Just to know that someone in leadership is taking his problem seriously is crucial to him.

(4) Be understanding. A listening ear is what many seek—just someone who will listen with both his heart and his ears. An effective leader identifies with people's needs and gives them the assurance that he understands. Problems evaporate in an atmosphere of understanding and love.

(5) Keep the problem small.
"My life is wrecked for good!"
"The church will not survive this problem!"

"I don't think I can make it."

"This problem is too big for me to handle."

Wait! The problem has taken on inaccurate proportions. It has gotten way out of bounds. It isn't nearly so bad as it looks.

Wise leadership offers positive hope in the face of any problem. God does have an answer. He is at work in all things to produce good, for He is the Creator. And this really is true. You can whittle a "huge problem" down to size by showing that God has an answer. Faith always knows a way out. No problem is insurmountable.

This is a key to problem solving: keep the problem small. For it really is in light of God's greatness.

(6) Be positive. Negativism is one of the most destructive forces in the church today. People are quick to say, "It can't be done . . . it's no use keeping on!" Leadership must counter with faith and vision.

People get caught in a "negativism syndrome." They become "problem-oriented," and life inverts and becomes a dread. Negativism is like poison. It destroys whatever it touches.

Stay on the positive side of every problem. View problems as opportunities—for they really are— opportunities in which God will work!

You have been called of God to be a deacon. It is a high and wonderful call. Rejoice and be glad that the Lord has by His grace granted to you this privilege.

Yes, you will face many problems. There will be times of fear and doubt. But Christ has assured you that with His call come the necessary resources by which the call is fulfilled.

Have a thankful heart. It is good that the Lord has singled you out to be a deacon.

NOTES ON CHAPTER 1

NOTES ON CHAPTER 1

NOTES ON CHAPTER 2

NOTES ON CHAPTER 2

NOTES ON CHAPTER 3

NOTES ON CHAPTER 3

NOTES ON CHAPTER 4

NOTES ON CHAPTER 4

NOTES ON CHAPTER 5

NOTES ON CHAPTER 5

NOTES ON CHAPTER 6

NOTES ON CHAPTER 6